Basic Quiltmaking Techniques

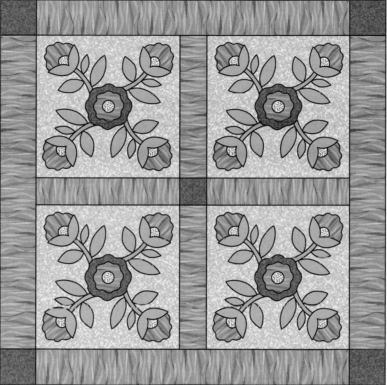

for Machine Appliqué

Maurine Noble

Martingale
& COMPANY

Bothell, Washington

Dedication

To all of my past, present, and future students. You make my teaching exciting, stimulating, and mentally rewarding.

Acknowledgments

My sincere thanks go to:

Carol Doak, for her great idea for this basic quiltmaking series.

Ursula Reikes, for asking me to write the book and for her continuing help and support.

The staff at Martingale & Company, for their enthusiasm and expert advice.

Christine Barnes, my editor, for putting it all together.

June Kendall, who, many years ago, showed me how to do the upside-down appliqué technique.

And to my husband, Ed Noble, for his continuing loving support.

Library of Congress Cataloging-in-Pubication Data
Noble, Maurine,
    Basic quiltmaking techniques for machine appliqué / Maurine Leander Noble.
        p. cm.
    ISBN 1-56477-241-1
    1. Patchwork quilts. 2. Machine appliqué. I. Title.
TT835.N627 1998
746.46—dc21   98-28905
                                            CIP

Credits

President	Nancy J. Martin
CEO/Publisher	Daniel J. Martin
Associate Publisher	Jane Hamada
Editorial Director	Mary V. Green
Technical Editor	Christine Barnes
Design and Production Manager	Cheryl Stevenson
Text Designer	Kay Green
Cover Designer	Magrit Baurecht
Copy Editor	Liz McGehee
Illustrator	Robin Strobel
Photographer	Brent Kane

Basic Quiltmaking Techniques
for Machine Appliqué
© 1998 by Maurine Leander Noble

Martingale & Company
PO Box 118
Bothell, WA 98041-0118 USA

Printed in the United States of America
03 02 01 00 99 98   6 5 4 3 2 1

Contents

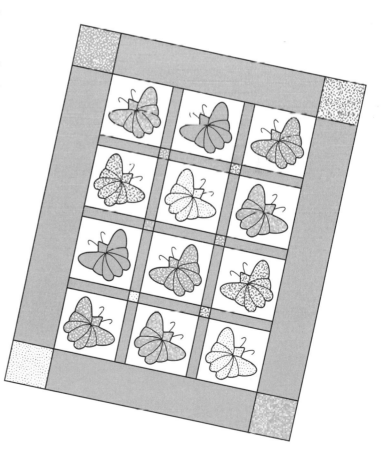

Foreword

Appliqué offers many design opportunities for your patchwork projects, and stitching the appliqué pieces by machine is yet another avenue for expressing your creativity. I am so pleased that Maurine Noble will introduce you to her easy techniques for machine appliqué.

Maurine's machine-sewing expertise is well known through her teaching and best-selling book, *Machine Quilting Made Easy,* and her recent book, *Machine Quilting with Decorative Threads*, which she co-authored with Elizabeth Hendricks (Martingale & Company). Now you will have the opportunity to build on the information you learned in *Your First Quilt Book (or it should be!)* with one of the best. Her knowledge of machine-sewing techniques will provide you with all the information you need to achieve success with machine appliqué.

Maurine has selected three methods of machine appliqué—fused, blind, and upside-down—and designed eight charming projects geared just to beginning quiltmakers. More experienced quiltmakers will enjoy the many details and helpful tips offered along the way.

I have no doubt that the information on the following pages will serve you well in your future machine-appliqué projects. Enjoy the techniques and have fun with the process!

Carol Doak

Preface

Appliqué is a needle art that has traditionally been done by hand. You'll find many examples of hand appliqué in antique and contemporary textiles, ranging from table linens and bedding to clothing embellishment and art quilts. In the past, hand-appliquéd quilts were often made to use leftover scraps from other sewing projects. Today, hand appliqué is a popular method of creating designs for both traditional and contemporary quilts. With knowledge and awareness of your sewing machine's abilities, and practice with patience, you can adapt most hand-appliqué designs to the sewing machine.

In the past few years, machine-appliqué techniques have become as accepted as machine-quilting techniques. Machine appliqué is fun to do, and there are as many ways to accomplish appliqué by machine as there are teachers teaching the subject. My goal has always been to do on the sewing machine what others do by hand, and machine appliqué is one of my favorite things to do.

When you become good friends with your sewing machine, anything is possible, but it does take practice. Be patient with yourself. Each appliqué you do will be better than the last. Challenge yourself and your sewing machine to an appliqué project!

Maurine Noble

Introduction

On the following pages, we will explore three basic techniques for machine appliqué: fused, blind, and upside-down appliqué. Many more techniques for machine appliqué exist, but these three will give you a good foundation and the skills needed to master any appliqué design on your sewing machine. I am not sure of the origin of these methods, but each time I do a project, I discover another variation or change that makes the technique even easier.

Think of appliqué as a technique for developing a picture on fabric. You have several options for creating that picture: If you would like your picture to look as if it were done by hand, the blind method is the one for you. If a stained-glass look is what you envision, the upside-down method, finished with black satin stitching, is perfect. When you choose to create a picture with many small pieces, the fused method is best.

The projects in this book have been chosen with you, the beginning quilter, in mind. The designs are simple; only a few fabrics and pattern pieces are required for each project. Once you've completed these projects, you'll have the skills you need to make an appliqué picture from any design or pattern you choose.

As in the other books in the Basic Quilt-making Techniques series, three symbols appear throughout to give you important information:

Tip boxes include handy hints that will make a process or technique a bit easier. Read these right away!

Alert boxes will let you know when you need to be careful. Your guardian angel will alert you so you don't make a common mistake.

Down the Road (DTR) boxes contain information that will come in handy on future projects, after you have some quiltmaking experience. You don't need this information right away, though, so feel free to ignore the Down the Road boxes until you're ready to explore a bit more.

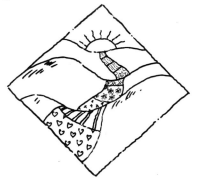

Read the entire book, especially the instructions for each appliqué method, before you begin any of the practice pieces or projects. I suggest that you try one project using each of the three techniques. You'll perfect your machine skills and quickly discover which method you like best. Best of all, you'll have fun while you learn!

Pattern and Design Sources

Let's begin with a common question from quilters new to machine appliqué: "Where do you find design ideas?" The answer is, everywhere! Traditional and contemporary appliqué patterns are available in quilt books and as packaged patterns. In many cases, you can combine appliqué pieces or shapes from books or patterns in various ways to make the design more your own. The "Rose of Sharon" pattern on pages 65 and 66 is an example of combining pattern elements.

There are other wonderful resources you can explore to find the perfect pattern for machine appliqué. When my children were very young, I delighted in embellishing their clothing with appliqués, often to cover a hole or tear. Most of the designs I used were favorite characters found in story and coloring books. These books contain simple line designs with a minimum of detail. Be aware, however, that you cannot copy exactly a trademarked or copyrighted design.

Dover books contain copyright-free designs that can be adapted for appliqué. If a design has more detail than you want, eliminate lines or simplify the design until it is usable. In the following example, I eliminated all but a few of the interior lines in the stained-glass butterfly design to make one that's suitable for a simple machine appliqué.

Butterfly from *Art Nouveau Stained Glass Pattern Book* (Dover Publications, Inc.)

Simplified and redrawn butterfly

You will also get design inspiration from unexpected sources. Magazine and newspaper ads, greeting cards, book illustrations, and catalogs are just a few of the places where you might see elements you can develop into designs. Consider cutting out figures or motifs printed on

fabric and appliquéing them onto a background fabric. This traditional technique is called *broderie perse*.

You can also adapt hand- or machine-quilting designs for appliqué. A simple feather quilting design, for example, can become an appliqué design if you separate the shapes. A flower-and-leaf quilting design might also become an appliqué design.

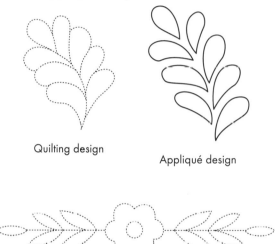

Quilting design

Appliqué design

Quilting design

Once you find a design, you must make it the right size for your project. Years ago, I enlarged or reduced designs by drawing them on graph paper, but now a copy machine does the job for me. It is easy to trace a design, make changes, and reduce or enlarge it on a copy machine. You may want to change the dimensions of a traditional appliqué pattern or quilting design to fit your background block, and you can also do this on a copy machine.

It's best to use simple shapes when practicing the techniques presented in this book. I simplify shapes in my beginning machine appliqué classes by rounding off pointed corners to make smooth curves, such as the tips of the leaves in "Tulip Time" on page 44. This change eliminates the stress of making perfect points on a first-time project. Very small appliqué pieces are difficult to handle; avoid them in your first projects. With practice, you'll soon realize that you can appliqué a shape as complicated as a running dog, using any of the methods explained on the following pages.

Fabric Selection

Quilt shops are full of wonderful fabrics that look like basket weave, flowers, leaves, sky, water, house siding, bricks, fur, or any texture you might want to depict. Once you begin to think "appliqué," you will find yourself looking for special fabrics to use in your projects. For several years, I have collected flower fabrics with large, splashy waves of color. It's nice to have what I need, when I need it, and it's a great excuse for building my stash. Save your scraps from other projects, as there are sure to be pieces you can use in appliqué.

Background Fabrics

Your background fabric should be a lighter or contrasting color to show off the appliqué pieces. Tone-on-tone prints make nice background fabrics, bringing softness and a sense of motion to a design. Textured or hand-dyed fabrics also lend subtle interest to the background.

 Cut the background fabric squares 1" to 1½" larger than the finished block size. This extra fabric allows for changes that may occur while you are working on the appliqué, extra fabric to trim if the edges ravel, and room to center the appliqué. After you finish and press the appliqué, trim the block to the finished size plus a ¼" seam allowance on all sides.

Appliqué Fabrics

Choose 100%-cotton fabrics for your appliqué. Cotton holds its shape and retains a crisp edge, necessary qualities for successful appliqué. You may, however, find it appropriate and fun to use a piece of velour for a fuzzy animal, organdy for a fish bowl or vase, or lamé for a shiny star. Unusual or glitzy fabrics can add pizzazz and intriguing texture to appliqué. Tone-on-tone prints add a dimension that you can't achieve with solid-colored fabrics.

If you choose a dark fabric for the background and a light fabric for the appliqué, you will probably need to line the appliqué fabric so the dark background does not show through. Try various lining fabrics, such as another layer of the appliqué fabric, white fabric, or muslin. Lay the appliqué fabric, with the lining fabric underneath, on the background fabric to see if it shows. Treat the appliqué and lining fabrics as one when you make the appliqué pieces.

There will be times when the wrong side of a fabric will be just what you are looking for, usually because it is lighter. Make it a habit to check the wrong side of your fabrics to consider the possibilities.

Contrasting colors, value variations, and a change in the scale of the prints you choose will make your finished appliqué more interesting.

Fussy Cutting

Consider using portions of large-scale prints or hand-dyed fabrics for a specific color or texture. To find the perfect area in the print, make a window by cutting the appliqué shape from the paper pattern, leaving the surrounding paper. Move the window on the fabric to audition areas for that appliqué shape.

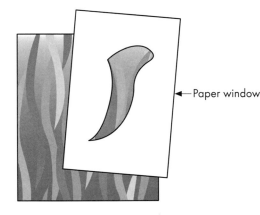

Paper window

Cutting appliqué pieces from specific sections of the fabric is called "fussy cutting." The remaining fabric will end up looking like a mouse has been nibbling, making holes throughout the piece.

Fabric Grain

Some appliqué patterns instruct you to trim the background fabric behind each appliqué piece. If you do this step, it's important to cut the fabric for each appliqué piece on the same grain as the background fabric. In the machine methods we will be using in this book, you leave the background fabric intact, so the appliqué pieces can be cut in any direction, on any grain of the fabric. This freedom allows you to take advantage of the color and print changes in your fabric without thinking about keeping the pieces on the straight grain.

Sample Blocks

When your quilt top requires several identical blocks, complete one block before cutting the pieces for all of the blocks. Or, make a mock-block by cutting finished-size pieces from your fabrics and pasting them on paper. Once you see your mock-block, you may want to make changes in the fabrics or the placement of the pieces. Now is the time to make those decisions, before you stitch.

Basic Tools and Supplies

You'll need a few general tools and supplies for machine appliqué. The special supplies needed for each appliqué method are listed with the step-by-step instructions.

Fine-point permanent marker. Use this marker to trace the pattern for all three appliqué methods.

Iron and ironing board. You'll need your iron and ironing board to press your appliqué pieces and fuse adhesive and stabilizer to your fabrics.

Pins. Flat pins, such as flower-headed pins, make it easy to pin appliqué pieces in place. The appliqué will also stay flat when you machine stitch it. (Never machine stitch over a pin; remove it before you stitch that area.)

Paper and fabric scissors. Be sure to use paper scissors to cut fusible web and freezer paper. Save your good scissors for fabric.

Appliqué scissors. These are helpful when trimming fabric close to the stitching line in the upside-down method.

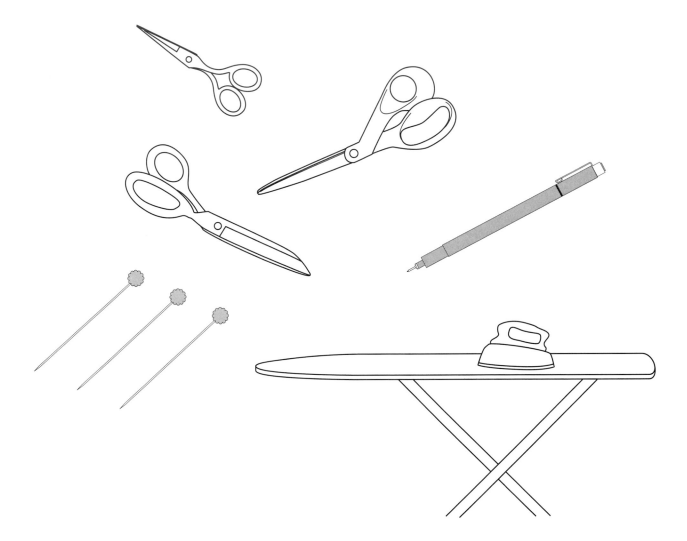

Appliqué Methods

Let's take a look at the three methods of machine appliqué: fused, blind, and upside-down. Each has its advantages and disadvantages, and I encourage you to practice all three techniques to discover which one you like best.

Fused Appliqué

Fused appliqué uses an iron-on adhesive to adhere the fabric pieces to the background fabric, holding them in place until you cover or secure the raw edges with stitching. The iron-on adhesive stiffens the appliqué, making this method less than ideal for a soft and cuddly quilt, but great for wall quilts and designs with many small pieces.

Supplies

Many iron-on adhesives are available, each with its own desirable and undesirable qualities. Following are descriptions of the different materials:

Paper-backed fusible web. Brand names of some of these popular fusing materials are HeatnBond, Steam-A-Seam, Steam-A-Seam 2 Double Stick, and Wonder-Under.

Fusible-web adhesive without backing. Fine-Fuse and Stitch Witchery are two readily available kinds.

Water-soluble fusible web. Sol-U-Web is the one I use.

Each product is slightly different in the way it feels and the way it is used. Several brands of fusing agents offer heavy and lightweight versions. Steam-A-Seam 2 Double Stick is sticky on both sides, so you can position the web on the wrong side of the appliqué fabrics. You can also position the pieces on the background fabric, moving them until you are happy with the placement, then press them permanently in place. Fusible web that is not attached to a pa-

per backing must be ironed onto the wrong side of the fabric using a Teflon sheet or pressing paper between the web and the iron. (The web alone will stick to the iron and make a mess that is difficult to remove.)

With heavy use and washings, some fusible webs do not stay adhered to the fabric. Placing a damp press cloth over the fused appliqué and pressing it dry may produce a longer-lasting seal. For the projects in this book, you will secure the raw edges with stitching.

Experiment with several fusing agents, following the directions for each product carefully. The temperature settings vary, as does the use of a steam or a dry iron, with different brands. Decide for yourself which one you like best—they all do a good job when used correctly.

Step-by-Step Fusing

Use the one-piece bird appliqué on the following page to experiment with an iron-on fusible web. Follow the directions on the package carefully. You can use this sample bird later to practice satin stitching.

1. Place a piece of paper-backed fusible web, paper side up, on top of the bird pattern. Using a fine-point permanent marker, trace the bird pattern onto the paper side of the fusible web.

If the design is directional, be sure to trace a mirror image of the pattern. For example, imagine the letter "R." To make it read correctly when fused, you must trace it onto the web backwards. The finished appliqué will then be facing in the right direction. In the case of this bird, it doesn't matter in which direction it faces; there is no right or wrong. It's best to trace it as it is printed to make it easy to follow the satin-stitching directions that begin on page 27.

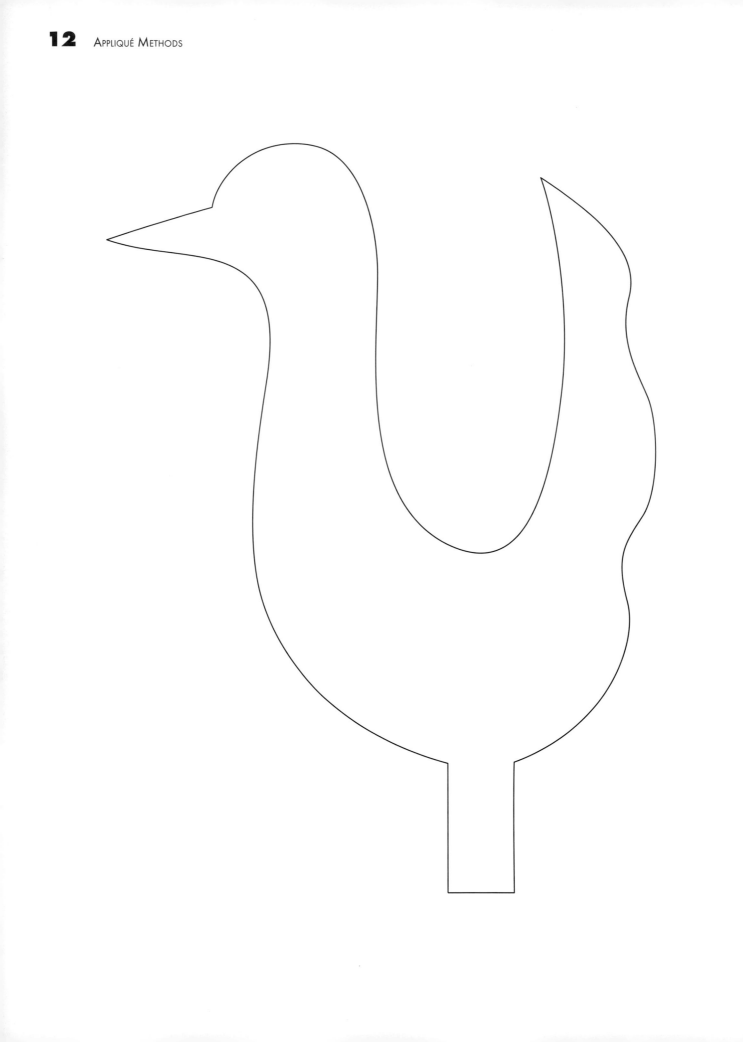

2. Cut the paper-backed fusible web around the traced bird, leaving a generous allowance.

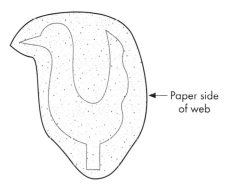

Paper side
of web

3. Preheat your iron to the setting required for the paper-backed fusible web you are using. Place the cut bird, paper side up, on the wrong side of the appliqué fabric. Press as directed in the instructions.

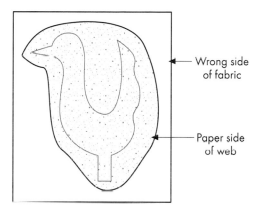

Wrong side
of fabric

Paper side
of web

Check to see if the bird is adhered to the fabric. If there are bubbles on the right side of the fabric, press on that side, too.

4. Allow the piece to cool and cut out the bird on the traced line. Peel away the paper backing.

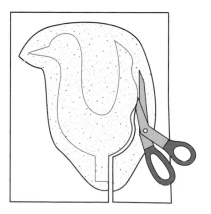

If the paper backing is difficult to remove from the fabric edges, use a straight pin to loosen one edge and separate the paper and fabric. The paper will then pull off easily.

5. Place the bird, right side up, on a 7" x 9" piece of background fabric. Press.

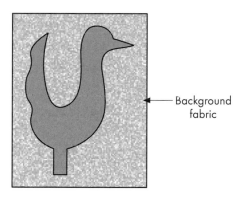

Background
fabric

You now have a sample to practice satin stitching inside and outside curves, corners, and points. For instructions, turn to page 27.

You can adapt this method to complicated designs composed of many pieces. When an appliqué pattern has multiple pieces, try Steam-A-Seam 2 Double Stick. The sticky backing is very helpful for holding small pieces in place until you are ready to press for permanent placement.

Blind Appliqué

This method of machine appliqué gives you a finished piece that looks as though it has been hand done. It may take a few practice pieces for you to be satisfied with the results, but be patient and give yourself time to perfect the technique. The "Heart-to-Heart Table Runner," "Butterflies" quilt, and "Tulip Time" wall hanging are all done using the blind-appliqué method. To learn this technique, begin with large, simple shapes, such as the tulip shown on page 61. As your skills increase, you can confidently tackle shapes with points or sharp curves.

Supplies

Some of the supplies you need for blind appliqué can be found around the house:
- 10" x 10" square of freezer paper
- Knitting needle
- Water-soluble stabilizer, such as Avalon, Aqua-Solv, or Solvy
- Water-soluble thread (optional), such as Stitch Away or Wash Away. (See the Tip with step 4 on page 16.)
- Invisible thread (.004mm), clear or smoke
- Sewing machine with adjustable blind-hem stitch or adjustable zigzag stitch
- Size 70/10 Sharp or Denim sewing-machine needles
- Open-toe embroidery foot or quilter's ¼" foot

Open-toe embroidery   Quilter's ¼" foot
foot

- 11½" x 11½" square of background fabric
- Fat quarters, small pieces, or scraps for appliqué

Before you begin, look closely at your design. The tulip on the following page is symmetrical, or balanced, meaning it is the same on both sides of an imaginary center line. Because the leaves and outer petals are mirror images of each other and go in opposite directions, you will need to make a pattern for each leaf and petal.

When a pattern is asymmetrical, such as the "Rose of Sharon" on page 66, the entire finished appliqué will be a mirror image of the pattern. To make the finished appliqué look exactly like the pattern, you must reverse all of the pieces before you trace them onto the freezer paper. To flop a design, turn the pattern over and, placing it on a window or a light table, trace the design on the back side. Use this side when you trace the pattern pieces onto the freezer paper.

If an appliqué piece, such as the outside petal on the tulip, will tuck under another piece, such as the center petal, you must add a ¼" seam allowance to the area that will be tucked under.

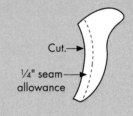

Cut. →

¼" seam
allowance →

Step-by-Step Blind Appliqué

1. Using a pen or pencil on the dull, unwaxed side of the freezer paper, trace around one leaf and one outer flower petal (with extended seam allowance), allowing enough space to fold the paper over onto itself. (By folding the paper, you can cut two pattern pieces at the same time, one in each direction.) Trace the flower center on a separate piece of freezer paper. Number the pieces to help you keep them in order.

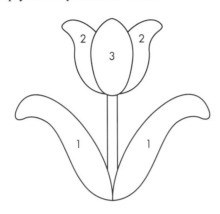

Note: At this point, don't be concerned with the stem of the tulip. We will make it later, using a different method.

2. Fold the freezer paper so that you can cut two of each piece at the same time. With paper scissors, cut out the pieces on the traced lines.

B-1

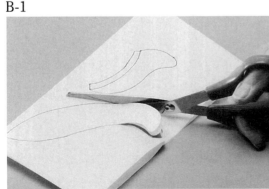

You can cut as many as four layers of freezer paper successfully at one time. Staple or pin the layers together to hold them securely.

3. Position the freezer-paper pattern pieces, shiny side down, on the wrong side of the fabric for each appliqué piece. Allow at least ¼" of extra fabric around each piece. Press the freezer paper to the wrong side of the fabric.

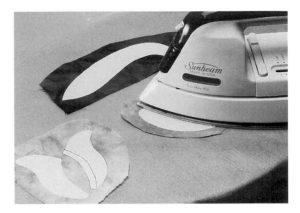

4. Cut a piece of water-soluble stabilizer a bit larger than each freezer-paper pattern and piece of fabric. Place the stabilizer on the right side of the appliqué fabric. You may want to pin the layers together to prevent them from slipping.

If you are a perfectionist and want no trace of thread on the turned edge of the appliqué, use water-soluble thread, such as Stitch Away or YLI Wash A Way. However, be aware that this thread may be more difficult to use than invisible thread and can break easily, causing frustration. Remember to change to invisible thread when appliquéing the shape to the background fabric.

5. Prepare your sewing machine with a size 70/10 Sharp or Denim needle, quilter's ¼" foot or open-toe embroidery foot, and water-soluble thread or invisible thread on the top and in the bobbin. With the water-soluble stabilizer on the bottom, stitch with short straight stitches (1.5mm stitch length) just outside the edge of the freezer-paper pattern. If the pattern piece has a ¼" extension so it can be tucked under another piece, as the outer tulip petals do, leave that area open and stitch around the rest of the piece, beginning and ending with a backstitch.

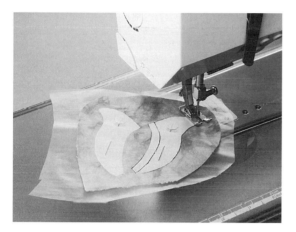

If the pattern piece does not have an added ¼" extension, stitch all the way around the piece.

If the water-soluble stabilizer shifts when you stitch around the appliqué piece, place a flat-headed pin through the freezer paper, fabric, and stabilizer. This will hold the layers together while you stitch.

6. With fabric scissors, trim the excess fabric and water-soluble stabilizer, leaving a scant ¼" seam allowance. Clip into the seam allowance at several places on all concave (inside) curves and trim the bulk from the points.

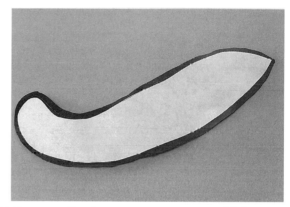

7. Remove the freezer-paper pattern. If the stitching goes all the way around the pattern, make a 1" to 1½" slit in the water-soluble stabilizer and turn the piece right side out through the slit.

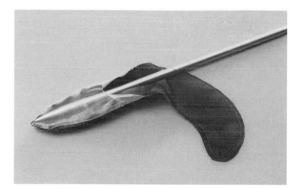

If you cut a slit that is too long, the appliqué will lose its shape when you turn it right side out.

If the appliqué piece has an extended ¼" seam allowance, turn it through the unstitched opening.

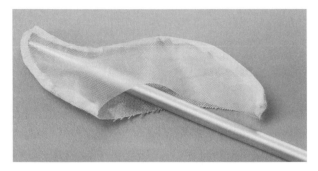

 Use a blunt-tipped knitting needle to help turn a long, narrow piece, such as the tulip leaf.

8. Smooth the curves and outside edges of the appliqué piece by carefully pushing the blunt point of the knitting needle around the stitching line. Position the point on the stitching line, within the fold of the fabric, not against the water-soluble stabilizer. A straight pin will help to pull out the points or sharp curves.

9. Lightly press the right (fabric) side of the turned appliqué piece with a steam or dry iron on the cotton setting. Do not press directly on the water-soluble stabilizer.

 Be sure that the seams are completely smoothed out before pressing. The water-soluble stabilizer will shrink slightly, helping to pull the seam line to the back of the appliqué piece. Once you press, it is not possible to adjust the seam line.

Stems

When all the appliqué pieces are stitched, turned, and pressed, it's time to make the stem. A stem is a narrow piece of fabric, straight or curved, with the raw edges turned under. You can use these pieces for stems, branches, Celtic curves, or any line in an appliqué design.

To make a curved stem, cut the fabric on the bias grain. For a straight stem, you can cut the fabric on the straight or bias grain. The following method is simple and gives you a perfect stem, regardless of the finished width.

1. Cut a length of stem fabric an inch or so longer than the appliqué pattern piece. The width of the fabric for the stem must be two times the finished stem width plus ½" (for two ¼" seam allowances). The finished stem width in this example is ½", so you must cut the piece 1½" wide. For one stem, you will need a 1½" x 5" piece.

If the stem is bias and will be curved, press it into the curve at this time.

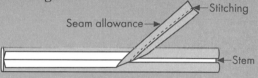

5. Open the stitched stem and carefully cut off the seam allowances, trimming away the stitching line.

You now have a perfect stem, with the raw edges turned under, ready to position on your background fabric and stitch in place.

If you are making several blocks in the same pattern, measure the total length of stem needed and make it all at one time.

2. Fold the strip in half lengthwise, with right sides facing out and wrong sides together; do not press. Stitch the entire length of the strip, using a ¼"-wide seam allowance.

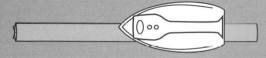

3. Open the tube, using a knitting needle to get it started, and press the ¼" seam allowances open in the center of the strip.

4. Turn the strip over and give it a good pressing on the right side to make crisp, folded edges.

For a very narrow stem, you can stitch a folded bias strip directly onto the background fabric.

1. Start by stitching the stem the desired distance from the folded edge. Trim the excess fabric very close to the stitching.

2. Press the fabric fold to cover the stitching and raw edges.

3. Blind-hem stitch in place, using invisible thread. (See the following page for instructions.)

Positioning the Pieces

Now you're ready to position the tulip shapes on your background fabric in preparation for appliqué.

1. Fold and press a square of background fabric, 11½" x 11½", twice diagonally to mark the center placement lines.

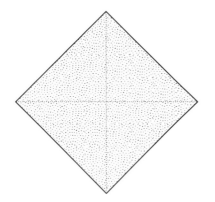

2. Loosely pin the stem and appliqué pieces in place on the background fabric. If the background fabric is a light color, you will be able to slide the pattern under the fabric and see the outline of the shapes through the fabric. You can also measure, placing the appliqué pieces equidistant from the folds in the background fabric.

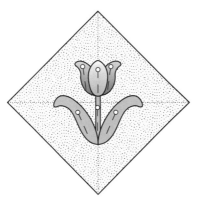

3. Remove the pieces one at a time and trim the water-soluble stabilizer from the back of each piece. Leave the stabilizer in the seam-allowance area only. Repin each trimmed piece.

If you used water-soluble thread to make the appliqué pieces, be sure to remove it from the sewing machine now.

Stitching the Appliqué

1. Thread the machine with lightweight, clear (for light- to medium-colored fabric) or smoke (for medium- to dark-colored fabric) invisible thread in the bobbin and needle. If you can change the needle position on your machine's blind-hem stitch, you will be able to use a ¼" quilter's foot if the needle hole in the foot is 1mm wide. If not, use the open-toe embroidery foot.

   Set the blind-hem stitch and test it on a scrap of fabric. Loosen the thread tension to one number lower than normal because the invisible thread is stretchy. If the stitch pulls too tightly on the appliqué edge, loosen the top tension another half or whole number.

It is important to use a fine, sharp needle in your machine (size 60/8, or 70/10 Sharp or Denim). A fine needle will ensure that your blind-hem stitch is as invisible as possible. The invisible thread can be nylon or polyester and should be very lightweight (.004mm). Use the same invisible thread that you would use for machine quilting. The thread you buy at a quilt shop is usually lightweight. Avoid the heavy invisible thread (like stiff fishing line) sold at some fabric stores.

On computerized machines, the blind-hem stitch automatically sets the needle position to the far right. If you can alter this setting, move the needle position to the center, then set the stitch length at .8mm and the stitch width at .8mm or narrower.

These numbers will vary with different machines. If you cannot alter your machine to stitch a very short, narrow blind-hem stitch, alter the zigzag stitch to short and narrow, with the length at 1mm and the width at .8mm.

An alternative is an altered buttonhole stitch. Engage the mirror image, setting the stitch length at 2mm and the width at .8mm.

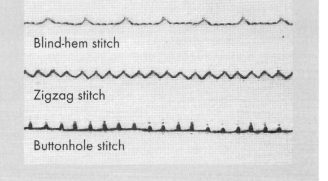

Blind-hem stitch

Zigzag stitch

Buttonhole stitch

Some brands of computerized machines will not allow a blind-hem stitch to be set less than 2mm in width. To override this setting, engage the twin-needle button and set the stitch width at 3mm and the length at 1mm. This setting will give you a tiny blind-hem stitch. Your machine may have a programmed appliqué stitch. If so, try it. With any of these choices, an open-toe embroidery foot gives you the visibility you need.

2. When you have adjusted the machine stitch and are satisfied with its size and tension, stitch around the appliqué pieces, fastening them to the background fabric. The straight stitches will be in the background fabric,

and the stitch that swings to the left will catch the appliqué piece and hold it in place. Remove the pin from each appliqué piece before you stitch over it. Stitch in this order: each side of the stem, completely around the leaves, the two outside petals, and the center petal.

3. If it is important to you to remove the remaining water-soluble stabilizer and water-soluble thread (if you used it in step 5, page 17), soak the appliqué in lukewarm water, rubbing it gently. Change the water several times until the stabilizer dissolves. Roll the appliqué in a clean towel to absorb the excess moisture. A final pressing on the back side of the background fabric will give you an appliqué that looks as if it were done by hand, with nothing between the appliqué and the background fabric.

4. Trim the appliqué square to the finished size plus a ¼" seam allowance on all sides.

You can do blind appliqué by substituting a lightweight interfacing or bridal tulle for the water-soluble stabilizer, but you will have better control using the water-soluble stabilizer. You may also find the extra layer of interfacing or tulle undesirable.

You can add a little loft to an appliqué shape. Using the freezer-paper pattern as a guide, cut a piece of low-loft batting the shape of the pattern piece. Tuck the batting behind the turned-under seam allowance and water-soluble stabilizer before stitching the appliqué piece in place.

Upside-Down Appliqué

This is a favorite method of machine appliqué because it gives you the freedom to add small pieces and details to a design. A satin stitch (a zigzag stitch adjusted to produce a solid line), programmed decorative stitch, or couching (stitching over ribbon floss, yarn, or other trim) is used to cover the raw edge of the appliquéd fabric, giving you the option of finishing the edge in any way that appeals to you. If you like a raw-edge look, it is perfectly all right to leave the edges unfinished.

With this technique, you stitch the appliqué pieces to the right side of the background fabric, working from the wrong side ("upside-down"). The design we will use to learn the technique, a variation of the "Rose of Sharon" pattern, requires four different fabrics: two for the flower rings, one for the flower center, and one for the stems and leaves.

Rose of Sharon

To make the flower appear to be on top of the stem, you will appliqué the stem and leaf fabric first. Next come the flower sections, starting with the outside ring and working toward the center. It's helpful to evaluate the design to determine the order in which the fabrics will be applied, then number the pieces.

Supplies

You'll find the supplies you need in quilt shops and at sewing-machine dealers. Iron-on, tear-away stabilizer (Press 'N Tear or Totally Stable) may be difficult to find, but don't substitute tear-away stabilizer that can't be ironed on. Mail-order sewing and notions catalogs carry iron-on, tear-away stabilizer. This stabilizer, which you press to the wrong side of the background fabric, serves two purposes: You use the stabilizer for tracing the appliqué design, just as you would with paper-backed fusible web. The stabilizer also holds the fabric taut when you do the satin stitching. You will remove the stabilizer after you complete the stitching.

For this practice piece, you will need:

• Press 'N Tear or Totally Stable iron-on, tear-away stabilizer

• Appliqué fabrics and background fabric (Scraps are probably fine for the smaller pieces.)

• Sewing machine with an adjustable zigzag stitch

• Darning foot for the first stitching and open-toe embroidery foot for satin stitching

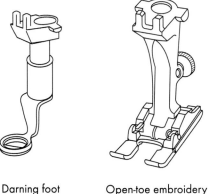

Darning foot   Open-toe embroidery
                              foot

• Size 70/10 or 80/12 Sharp, Denim, or 75/11 Embroidery sewing-machine needle

• Lightweight cotton or rayon machine-embroidery thread

• Appliqué scissors or small, sharp scissors

Step-by-Step Upside-Down Appliqué

1. Choose the fabrics for the appliqué pieces and the background.
2. Cut a piece of iron-on stabilizer at least 1" larger on all sides than the complete appliqué pattern.
3. On the rough side of the iron-on stabilizer, with a permanent pen or a pencil, trace the complete design. Note that there are no seam allowances.

Because you will be working from the back side of the fabric, the traced design will be reversed; that is, it will be a mirror image of the completed design. If you use this design as you see it on page 23, the stem will curve to the right on the stabilizer but to the left on the finished appliqué. If you want to flop a design so that it will look as it does on the original pattern, turn the pattern over and, placing it on a window or a light table, trace the design on the other side. Use that side when you trace the design onto the stabilizer.

4. Position the stabilizer pattern with the shiny side against the wrong side of the background fabric. Press, using the steam and cotton settings on your iron. Press the right side of the background fabric if bumps and bubbles occur where the iron-on stabilizer did not completely adhere.
5. Thread your sewing machine with lightweight machine-embroidery thread in the top and bobbin. Use a visible, but neutral, colored thread that can later be easily covered with a satin stitch. Attach a darning foot and drop or cover the feed dogs on your sewing machine. Set a straight stitch with the length and width at 0.

The thread in the bobbin will be the visible thread on the right side of the appliqué. Later, you will cover it with a satin stitch. If you use white, regular-weight sewing thread in the bobbin and plan to satin stitch with black, lightweight embroidery thread, you may find it difficult to cover the white thread with the satin stitching. To avoid this problem, use a lightweight, matching or neutral thread in the bobbin for the first stitching.

6. If your background fabric is a light color, hold it up to the light to see the marked pattern lines. Use these lines as a guide to place the green fabric so it covers the stem and leaves.

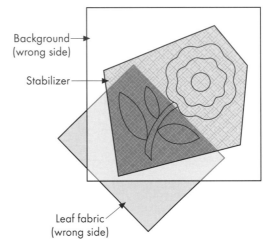

Background (wrong side)

Stabilizer

Leaf fabric (wrong side)

If the background fabric is a dark color, place pins around the stem and leaves to indicate where you need to place the green fabric.

Wrong side   Right side

7. Begin with the first fabric to be appliquéd, in this example, the green for the stem and leaves. Press the fabric and place it right side up on the right side of the background fabric. I have not found it necessary to pin the appliqué pieces in place when stitching with a darning foot.

8. Begin working on the stabilizer side. Using a darning foot with the feed dogs dropped and moving the fabric slowly to achieve a short stitch, free-motion stitch around the outline of the stem and leaf lines marked on the stabilizer. The appliqué fabric will be underneath, with the right side of the fabric against the bed of the machine.

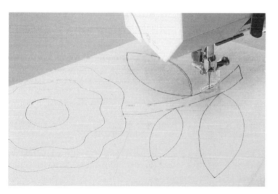

 If you are uncomfortable stitching free-motion with a darning foot, you can use a ¼" quilter's foot or open-toe embroidery foot with the feed dogs raised. There will be a tendency for the appliqué pieces to shift, so you will need to pin them in place. I encourage you to practice free-motion stitching with a darning foot. You will soon gain control, and once you learn to free-motion stitch comfortably, you can accomplish anything with your sewing machine.

 Do not turn the fabric when free-motion stitching with a darning foot. Think of the needle as a pencil, tracing around the pattern as you would when the paper is flat on a table.

9. Place the piece, right side up, on a flat surface. Lift the excess green fabric away from the background and trim close to the stitched line with a pair of appliqué scissors or small, sharp scissors. Appliqué scissors enable you to trim the fabric very close to the stitching line.

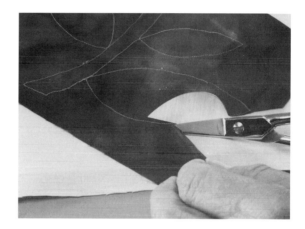

10. Next, free-motion stitch around the outer and inner lines of the outer flower piece. Trim the fabric.

11. Place, stitch, and trim the middle ring fabric. This piece will overlap the outer ring fabric slightly on the inner line, leaving only one raw edge to cover with satin stitching.

12. Place, stitch, and trim the center fabric.

There should never be more than one layer of appliqué fabric attached to the background fabric. With this pattern, you cut away the center area of each flower piece before adding the next. If you stitch and trim correctly, you will need to cover just one raw edge with satin stitching where two fabrics overlap slightly.

13. The appliqué is complete, with each design area covered by one fabric. Now it's time to finish the raw edges with a satin stitch on the right side. When satin stitching a design that has several appliqué pieces, satin stitch in the same order as you appliquéd the pieces. Each tie-off end will be covered by another line of satin stitching.

For this design, satin stitch as follows:

• Stitch each leaf, beginning and ending at the stem.

• Stitch the stem, beginning and ending at the end next to the flower.

• Stitch around each flower section.

See pages 27–31 for complete satin-stitching instructions. The iron-on stabilizer stays in place until you finish the satin stitching.

If you did not trim close enough to the straight stitching, there will be more than 2mm between the stitching and the raw edge. You will need to increase the width of the satin stitch to cover both the straight stitching and the raw edge. Or, trim a little closer to the straight stitching.

The iron-on stabilizer prevents the satin stitching from tunneling. Tunneling occurs when you zigzag one or two layers of fabric that are not stable enough to hold the threads taut. The zigzag stitch causes the fabric to tuck and pucker under the stitching. The wider the satin stitch, the more severe the tunneling. Using a stabilizer prevents this problem.

Satin Stitching

Satin stitching is a zigzag stitch shortened until the threads are so close together that they almost make a solid line. The width of this line is determined by the width that you set the needle swing or zigzag on your machine.

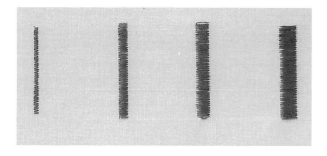

Supplies

The weight of the thread you use will make a difference in the look of the satin stitch. Lightweight, cotton machine-embroidery thread (DMC 50, Madeira Cotona 50 or 80, Mettler 60, Coats Lightweight Dual Duty or YLI Heirloom Cotton 70) will give a finer, smoother appearance than regular-weight sewing thread. Rayon thread (Madeira, Sulky, Coats, or another brand of 40-weight rayon) gives the satin stitch a sheen and richness, but it is a bit heavier.

You'll also need.

• Sharp or Denim sewing-machine needles in size 70/10 or 80/12 for lightweight, cotton machine-embroidery thread

• Embroidery needle in size 75/11 for rayon thread (This needle will prevent the thread from splitting and breaking.)

• 6½" x 8½" piece of Totally Stable or Press 'N Tear iron-on stabilizer to keep the satin stitching flat

• Open-toe embroidery foot

You'll need to practice outside and inside curves, corners, and points. Follow the directions that begin on page 11 to make the fused appliqué bird.

1. Press the iron-on stabilizer onto the wrong side of the background fabric.
2. Use your open-toe embroidery foot with the feed dogs engaged. You may use the same cotton or rayon thread in the bobbin as in the needle, or use a lightweight machine-embroidery bobbin thread in the bobbin.
3. In the background of the bird piece, or on a scrap with stabilizer, stitch a 3mm wide satin stitch, adjusting the stitch length until the stitch looks almost like a solid line. If the stitch is too short, the satin stitch will be too dense. If the stitch is too long, the satin stitch will not adequately cover the raw edge of the appliqué piece.
4. Loosen the thread-tension dial (move to a lower number) until you can see the top thread on the back of the satin stitching and cannot see any bobbin thread on the top. This adjustment gives you a satin stitch with an unbalanced tension, but it looks beautiful from the right side.

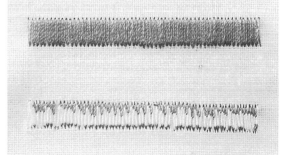

The narrower the zigzag, the more likely it is that the bobbin thread will be visible on the top. For a very narrow satin stitch, use the same color and weight of thread in the bobbin as on the top.

Straight Edges

1. Begin on the straight part of the inside tail, with 5 or 6 short straight stitches (.5 stitch length) to tie off the threads.

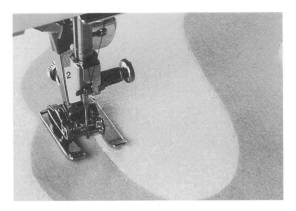

2. Switch to the zigzag setting that you determined looked best and begin satin stitching. The needle should just barely cover the appliqué fabric when it swings to the right. Most of the width of the satin stitch should be within the appliqué fabric. If you have the option to stop your machine with the needle in the fabric, set the needle to stop *down* for this exercise.

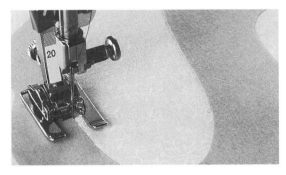

Inside Curves

The first curve you come to on the bird is the inside curve on the deepest part of the back.

1. Stitch toward the curve until the appliqué edge curves to the right and under the inside right edge of the presser foot. Stop with the needle on the inside of the satin stitch (left swing of the needle).

2. Raise the presser foot and pivot the fabric until the appliqué edge is parallel to the inside right edge of the presser foot.

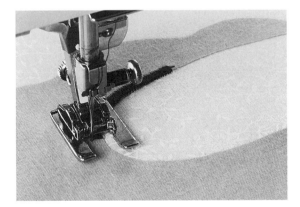

3. Stitch until the edge of the appliqué curves away again. Continue to pivot and stitch in the same manner until the inside curve is evenly stitched.
4. Continue stitching up the back of the neck.

Outside Curves

The next curve you come to is the back and top of the head.

1. Satin stitch around the outside curve until the edge of the appliqué begins to curve away from the inside right edge of the presser foot.

2. Stop with the needle in the background fabric on the edge of the curve (right swing of the needle). Raise the presser foot and pivot the piece so the edge of the appliqué fabric is parallel to the inside right edge of the presser foot.

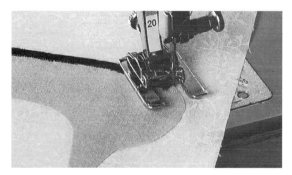

3. Lower the presser foot and continue stitching until the edge of the appliqué curves away again. Continue to pivot and stitch in the same manner until the outside curve is evenly stitched. On a sharp, tight curve you will need to pivot every 4 to 6 stitches.

If you satin stitch a curve without pivoting, the stitch will begin to look as if it is leaning sideways, especially on a tight curve. If you pivot with the needle on the wrong side, you will leave tiny gaps of fabric between the stitches.

Angles

Stitching around the outside curve of the head, you reach an angle where the beak begins. Stop with the needle on the left, raise the presser foot, and pivot so the presser foot is parallel to the edge of the appliqué. Continue stitching along the top edge of the beak.

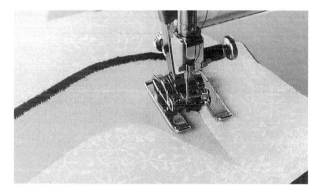

When tapering to a point, the needle position on your machine will determine the direction of the taper. For this exercise, the needle should be in the center position.

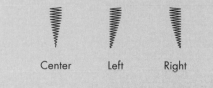

Center Left Right

Outside Points

The next challenge is the tip of the beak, an outside point.

1. Stitch toward the point. When the width of the satin stitch is the same as the width of the point, stop.

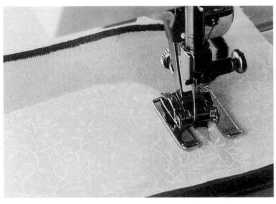

2. Pivot slightly to center the point of the beak in the opening of the presser foot. While slowly stitching, manually decrease the width of the satin stitch to match the decrease in the point. Your stitch width should be 0 at the tip of the beak.

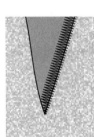

3. Pivot the piece.

4. Stitch away from the point, increasing the satin-stitch width to match the increase in the point. When the width is back to 3mm, continue to stitch along the lower beak and the front curve of the bird.

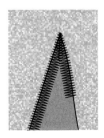

Inside Corners

The leg has an inside corner with a 90° angle.

1. Stitch to the corner; continue a distance equal to the width of the zigzag stitch.

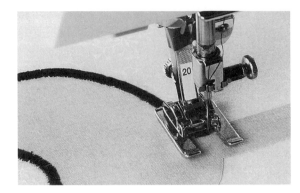

2. Stop with the needle on the right side of the swing, lift the presser foot, and pivot.

3. Raise the needle from the fabric; it will automatically swing to the left. Move the fabric to the left and place the needle into the same needle hole.

4. Continue stitching down the front of the leg.

Outside Corners

This is the final stitching maneuver.

1. Stitch until you have completely covered the lower corner of the leg. Stop with the needle on the left side of the swing.

2. Lift the presser foot and pivot. Raise the needle, rotate the fabric to the right, and place the needle into the same needle hole in the fabric.

Continue stitching. This method does not stitch over the corner twice, so it gives you a smooth, flat corner.

Tie-off

1. When you have satin stitched around the bird, completely covering the straight tie-off stitches at the beginning, stop with the needle down. Pivot the piece so you can stitch across the satin stitching.

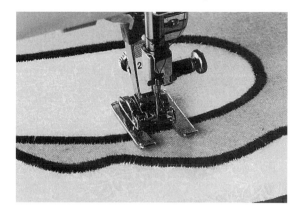

2. Raise the needle and change to the short straight stitch you used to tie off the threads at the beginning. Stitch across the satin stitching. The tie-off threads will bury themselves in the stitching.

Curves, points, and corners will occur in future appliqué projects. With practice, you will gain the confidence to masterfully stitch any appliqué shape.

Projects

Now that you're acquainted with the three methods of machine appliqué, you're undoubtedly eager to put your new skills to work on a machine appliqué project. This chapter contains eight projects, ranging from a simple pillow with a one-piece appliqué to a child's quilt with six animal appliqués. You might like to warm up with the pillow or table runner, and then move on to one of the more challenging projects.

Before you begin, let's review a few important points:

Read the instructions completely.

The cutting instructions direct you to cut your background pieces slightly larger than you normally would to center and trim the appliquéd block. Once you've completed the appliqué, trim each block to the size specified in the assembly instructions.

The background and border pieces are rotary cut. You can cut these pieces with scissors, but careful rotary cutting is fast and accurate.

The yardage requirements are based on 44"-wide fabric that has at least 42" of usable width. If your fabric has less than 42" of usable width, you may need to buy more fabric. The backing for "Butterflies," "Tulip Time," and "Rose of Sharon" is an exception; see the note with each project.

The materials lists specify colors to help you see which fabrics go where in my quilts, but feel free to use any colors you like to make the project truly your own. If you use different colors, try to choose fabrics that have a similar value (lightness or darkness) to the ones I have chosen.

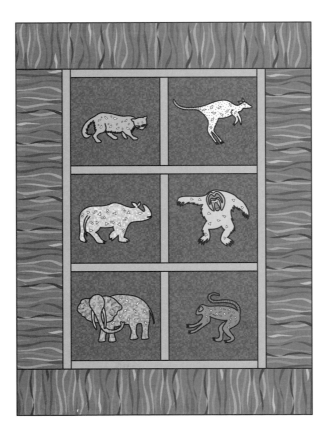

Kitty Cat Pillow

A project that requires only one block, such as the Kitty Cat pillow you see here, is perfect for beginners. This easy, one-piece appliqué requires only two design decisions from you: fabric colors and patterns, and the direction of the tail. As you can see in the photo on page 41, the figure is symmetrical except for the tail, which you can place on either side of the body.

Color photo on page 41.

Project Information at a Glance	
Finished Pillow Size:	16" x 16"
Finished Block Size:	11" x 11"
Finished Sashing Width:	½"

Materials: 44" wide fabric

⅜ yd. gold for background

¼ yd. gray textured print for kitty appliqué

7" x 10" piece of iron-on, tear-away stabilizer (Press 'N Tear or Totally Stable)

⅛ yd. black for sashing

⅝ yd. multicolored print for setting triangles and pillow backing

18" x 18" square of muslin for inside backing of block*

18" x 18" square of low-loft batting

16" x 16" pillow form

Safety pins

*The backing will be inside the pillow and will not be seen. Therefore, you can use any light-colored cotton fabric.

Cutting

Fabric	No. of Pieces	Size to Cut	2nd Cut	Placement
Gold	1	12½" x 12½"		Background
Gray	1	7" x 9"		Kitty appliqué
Black	2	1" x 11½"		Sashing
	2	1" x 12½"		Sashing
Multi	2	9" x 9"	◻	Setting triangles
	2	12" x 16½"		Pillow backing

◻ Cut the squares once diagonally.

Block Assembly

The following instructions are for the upside-down method. You can use the fused method (page 11) if you prefer.

1. Follow the directions for "Upside-Down Appliqué" on pages 22–26. Once you have free-motion stitched around the kitty outline, trim the excess fabric close to the stitching. Still working from the back of the piece, free-motion stitch the details on the kitty face, including the whiskers. (You will use this stitching as a guide to do the final stitching from the front.)

 Be sure to stitch the kitty outline and trim the excess fabric *before* stitching the details. If you stitch the lines for the whiskers before trimming the excess fabric, you will stitch the excess fabric to the background.

2. With the piece right side up, satin stitch over the cut edges, covering the straight stitching. Begin with the tail, then stitch the back legs, followed by the body. Using a darning foot with the feed dogs dropped or covered, stitch the eyes and nose with a free-motion zigzag stitch. Stitch the mouth and whiskers with a free-motion straight stitch, stitched back and forth several times.
3. Remove the iron-on, tear-away stabilizer from the wrong side of the block.
4. Press the block and trim it to 11½" x 11½", carefully centering the appliqué.

Pillow Assembly

1. Mark the midpoints on the sashing strips and opposite sides of the block. Pin the 1" x 11½" sashing strips to opposite sides of the block, matching the midpoints and ends. Stitch, using a ¼"-wide seam allowance. Add the 1" x 12½" sashing strips to the remaining sides of the block.

2. Mark the midpoints on the long edges of 2 setting triangles. Mark the midpoints on opposite edges of the block. Pin the triangles to the block, matching the midpoints; stitch. Repeat with the remaining triangles on the remaining sides of the block.

The long cut edge of each setting triangle is on the bias. When stitching a bias edge to a straight-grain edge, place the bias-edge piece on the underside. The feed dogs of your sewing machine will ease the fullness of the bias edge to the straight-grain edge, keeping the bias from stretching.

3. Layer the appliqué block, batting, and muslin or light-colored fabric square. Pin-baste.

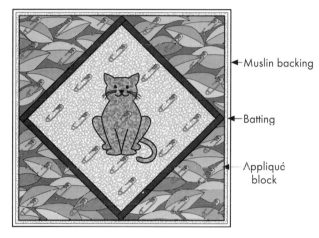

← Muslin backing

← Batting

← Appliqué block

4. Quilt by hand or by machine. I machine quilted the pillow on page 41 by free-motion stitching around the kitty. Then I stitched continuous loops in the background. Next, I stitched in-the-ditch on both sides of the sashing, using a walking foot. If you use a printed fabric for the setting triangles, you can quilt the design lines in the fabric with free-motion stitching.

5. Trim the excess fabric, batting, and muslin to 16½" x 16½".

6. On one long edge of each 12" x 16½" rectangle, turn under ½" twice and press. Machine stitch the edge.

7. Place a rectangle, right side down, on the pillow top; pin. Place the remaining rectangle, right side down, on the pillow top, overlapping the first rectangle; pin. Machine stitch around the edges, using a walking foot and a generous ¼"-wide seam allowance. Backstitch where the rectangles end to strengthen these stress points.

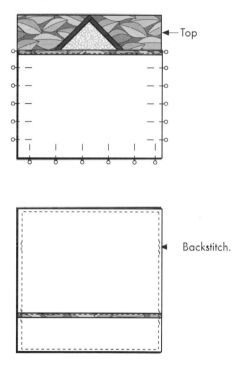

← Top

Backstitch.

8. Turn the pillow right side out and insert the pillow form. You're finished!

For a different look, add piping or a ruffle to the edge of the pillow.

Kitty Cat Pillow

Heart-to-Heart Table Runner

This table runner gives you the opportunity to practice the blind-appliqué method using a simple heart shape. The bias strip that curves along the length of the runner teaches you how to make floral stems or other narrow curved pieces. This project is also a great way to try out some of the programmed decorative stitches built into your sewing machine.

Project Information at a Glance	
Finished Runner Size:	17½" x 53"
Finished Heart Size:	5½" x 6"
Number of Hearts to Make:	7
Finished Width of Stem:	¾"

Materials: 44"-wide fabric

1⅝ yds. blue textured print for background and
    backing
¼ yd. yellow textured print for hearts
½ yd. multicolored print for stem
1 package water-soluble stabilizer (Solvy,
    Avalon, or Aqua-Solv)
Freezer paper
20" x 55" piece of lightweight cotton batting*

*I use a needlepunched cotton batting for a table runner because it does not transfer heat as readily as polyester batting. With this batting, the runner also lies flat on the table, and it doesn't require a lot of quilting.

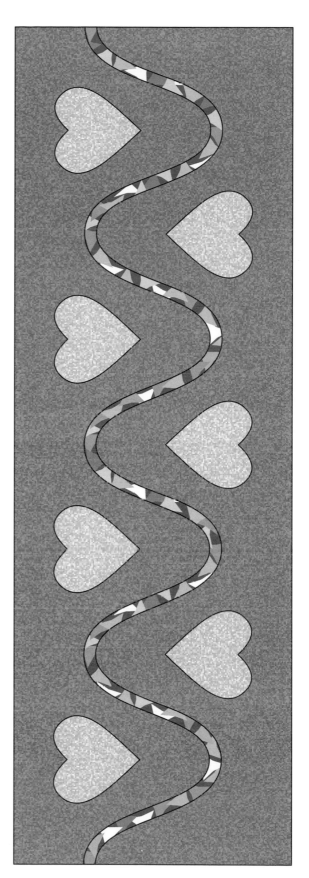

Color photo on page 42.

Cutting

Fabric	No. of Pieces	Size to Cut
Blue	1	19" x 54½"
	1	20" x 56"
Yellow	7	6" x 6½"
Stabilizer	7	6" x 6½"

Making Bias Strips

To create a stem that curves, cut and piece bias strips using this technique:

1. Fold the multicolored fabric on the diagonal at one end and press to mark a crease. Using the crease as a guide, cut 4 strips, each 2" wide, on the bias.

2. Join the strips with a ¼"-wide seam to make a 95"-long strip.

Join the bias strips.

Runner Assembly

1. Fold the 19" x 54½" background fabric in half lengthwise and press a crease. Fold the fabric in half crosswise 3 times, pressing creases as you fold. These folds will divide the fabric into 16 sections.

2. Using a saucer or other circular shape placed on each side of the lengthwise

crease, mark a curved design line with a chalk-wheel marker.

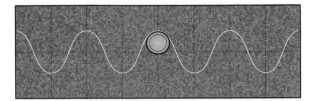

3. Fold and stitch the bias strip, following the directions for making stems on page 19. Press the bias strip to fit the curve in your design. The finished width of the strip will be ¾".

4. Pin the bias strip in place on the background fabric. Using invisible thread, stitch each folded edge to the background fabric with a narrow (.8mm) and short (.8 to 1mm) blind-hem stitch or small zigzag stitch.

5. Trace the heart pattern 3 or 4 times on the dull side of the freezer paper. Cut out the hearts.

You can reuse the freezer-paper pattern until it will no longer stick to the fabric when ironed.

6. Follow the directions for "Blind Appliqué" on pages 14–18 to make 7 hearts, using water-soluble stabilizer and invisible or water-soluble thread. Trim, turn, and press the hearts.

7. Cut away the excess water-soluble stabilizer and pin the hearts in place on the runner background. Stitch around each heart with a blind-hem stitch, using the same settings and thread as you did for the bias strip.

8. Trim the runner top to 18" x 53½".

If you want to embellish your hearts as you appliqué them, try a decorative stitch, such as a programmed machine feather stitch or buttonhole stitch. Use a heavy thread, such as Jeanstitch, other topstitching thread, or #12 pearl cotton with a 90/14 topstitching needle. See the small photo on page 42.

Finishing

1. Spread the batting on a tabletop. Place the pressed runner backing, right side up, on the batting, smoothing out any wrinkles. The runner top, wrong side up, goes on top of the backing and batting.

2. Pin the 3 layers together, placing straight pins at right angles to the outside edges.

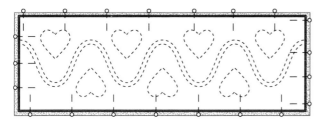

3. With a walking foot and cotton or polyester sewing thread, stitch the 3 layers ¼" from the edge of the runner top. Begin somewhere along the long edge, backstitching for ½" at the beginning. Stop and backstitch again when you are 12" from where you started.

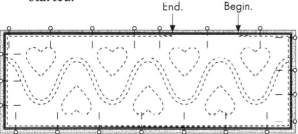

4. Change to a long stitch (5mm) and machine baste the remaining 12", ending where you began the stitching.

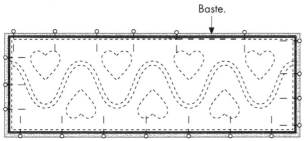

5. Trim the excess backing and batting, leaving a ¼"-wide seam allowance. Trim the corners to reduce the bulk.

6. Press the ¼"-wide seam allowance on the runner top in the basted area toward the center of the runner. Stitch the backing and batting together next to the pressed seam allowance. This step ensures a crisp edge when you turn the runner right side out.

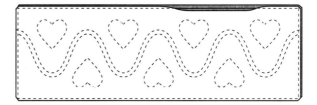

7. Remove the basting and turn the runner right side out through the 12" opening; pin the open edges. Continue pinning the edge all the way around the runner. Topstitch with a walking foot and matching thread as close to the turned edge as you can evenly stitch, removing the pins just before you reach each one and closing the 12" opening as you stitch.

8. Pin-baste with safety pins and quilt by hand or machine. I machine quilted the runner on page 42 along both edges of the bias strip and around each heart. Three additional quilting lines radiate from each heart. You may stitch these lines with a walking foot, using the edge of the foot as a stitching guide. If you feel confident, free-motion stitch around the hearts.

**Heart-to-Heart
Table Runner**
Heart
Cut 7

Gallery

Kitty Cat Pillow by Maurine Noble, 1998, Seattle, Washington, 16" x 16". Learn the upside-down method for a one-piece appliqué, and satin stitch the edges when you make this simple pillow. You can substitute another appliqué on the background square if you like.

Heart-to-Heart Table Runner
by Maurine Noble, 1998, Seattle, Washington, 17½" x 53". Blind appliqué is the ideal technique for making curved shapes with that hand-stitched look. A special technique for sewing bias strips ensures a near-perfect twining stem.

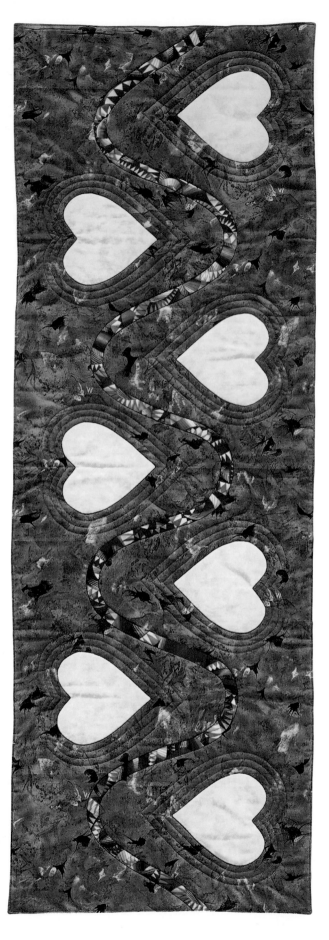

Feather stitching is one of many ways to embellish the edges of a simple appliqué.

Star-Spangled Night *by Maurine Noble, 1998, Seattle, Washington, 30" x 38". Practice stitching perfect points when you appliqué the moon and the stars on this simple wall quilt. The pieces are fused using adhesive web that's sticky on both sides.*

Tulip Time *by Maurine Noble, 1998,*
Seattle, Washington, 42½" x 42½". These easy-to-make
tulips are stitched using the blind-appliqué method.
Sashing and inner borders frame the on-point blocks.

Hand-dyed fabric, with its variations in color and
texture, is fun to use for floral appliqués.

*With the upside-down or blind method, you can use your
favorite programmed decorative stitches to finish the edges.*

Butterflies *by Maurine Noble, 1998, Seattle, Washington, 42½" x 53". Simple one-piece butterflies are well suited to the blind-appliqué technique. Use a buttonhole stitch to appliqué and embellish the edges at the same time.*

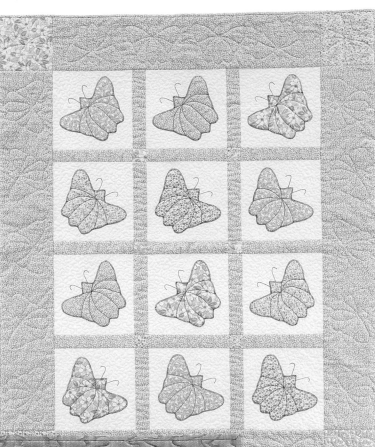

Butterfly Dance *by Maurine Noble, 1998, Seattle, Washington, 26¼ " x 26¼ ". Butterflies appear to dance on the background fabric in this contemporary version. Watercolor floral fabrics add to the light, airy design.*

Rose of Sharon *by Maurine Noble, 1998, Seattle, Washington, 43½" x 43½". The upside-down–appliqué method is ideal for designs that consist of many pieces. You can finish the edges with satin stitching, a decorative programmed stitch, or couching.*

Dream Creatures *by Maurine Noble, 1998, Seattle, Washington, 35½ " x 47". Create your own animal kingdom with these upside-down appliqués, then embellish them with a variety of decorative stitches.*

Coffee Break *by Maurine Noble, 1998, Seattle, Washington, 17½ " x 23". Make this whimsical wall quilt using the fused appliqué method. The steam is made of sparkle organdy, couched with ribbon floss.*

Coffee Break

The coffee-bean background fabric spoke to me! That's often the reason I buy a piece of fabric—because I really like it or it reminds me of someone special. This small quilt would look great on a kitchen wall. The steam shapes provide an opportunity to use iron-on fusible adhesive and to couch the edges. Couching is the technique of laying ribbon floss, yarn, or braid over a raw edge and stitching over it to cover the edge.

Color photo on page 48.

Project Information at a Glance	
Finished Quilt Size:	17½" x 23"
Finished Block Size:	9" x 14½"
Number of Blocks to Make:	1
Finished Inner Border Width	1"
Finished Outer Border Width	3"

Materials: 44"-wide fabric

⅓ yd. coffee-bean fabric for background*

Green fat quarter or scrap for cup and cornerstones

5" x 12" piece of sparkle organdy for steam

5" x 12" piece of paper-backed fusible web

⅛ yd. orange for inner border

⅜ yd. beige textured print for outer border and binding

⅝ yd. for backing (includes 8" for sleeve)

1½ yds. ribbon floss, yarn, or braid for couching

Large-eyed hand needle

20" x 25" piece of lightweight cotton batting

You will need ½ yd. if you use a directional fabric.

Cutting

Fabric	No. of Pieces	Size to Cut	Placement
Coffee bean	1	10½" x 16"	Background
Green	1	4" x 8"	Cup
	4	1½" x 1½"	Cornerstones
Orange	2	1½" x 15"	Inner border (sides)
	2	1½" x 9½"	Inner border (top & bottom)
Beige	2	3½" x 17"	Outer border (sides)
	2	3½" x 17½"	Outer border (top & bottom)
	2	2" x 42"	Binding

Block Assembly

1. Follow the directions for "Fused Appliqué" on pages 11–13 to trace, cut, and fuse the cup and steam pieces to the background fabric, starting with the cup. Lay the steam over the back rim; then satin stitch the front rim to cover the raw edges of the steam.

2. Follow the directions on page 27 to satin stitch the outside edges of the coffee cup, rim, and saucer, leaving the back rim unstitched under the steam.

3. Trim the block to 9½" x 15", carefully centering the appliqué.

Quilt Assembly

1. Stitch the 1½" x 15" inner border strips to the sides of the block. Stitch a 1½" x 1½" cornerstone to each end of the 1½" x 9½" inner border strips. Add the strips to the top and bottom of the block, matching the corner seams.

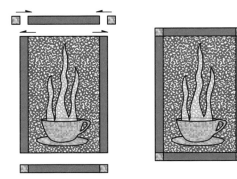

2. Add the 3½" x 17" outer border strips to the sides of the block, followed by the 3½" x 17½" border strips to the top and bottom.

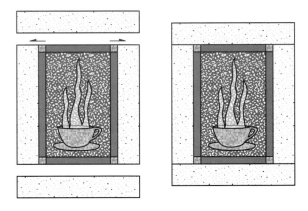

3. To couch the edges of the steam pieces, I used an iridescent ribbon floss that looks just like the sparkle organdy. Using your open-toe embroidery foot, couching foot, or braiding foot and invisible thread, zigzag the ribbon floss in place, covering the raw edges of the organdy. Set the zigzag stitch width to equal the width of the ribbon floss. Begin and end the couching with a few short straight stitches to tie off the invisible threads.

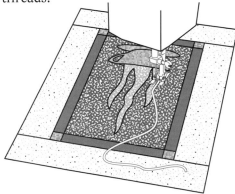

4. Using a large-eyed hand needle, bring the ends of the ribbon floss to the back of the quilt top. Tie the ribbon ends with the bobbin thread and clip 1" tails. The tails will be covered by the batting and backing.

Finishing

1. Layer the quilt top with batting and backing; pin-baste.
2. Quilt by hand or machine. I outline-quilted the cup, steam, and inner border of the quilt on page 48, then quilted wiggly lines in the background to suggest steam.
3. Attach the binding, add a sleeve, fix yourself a cup of coffee, and admire your wall quilt.

1
Coffee Break
Cup
Cut 1

2
Coffee Break
Steam
Cut 1

Butterflies

This appliqué pattern comes from a block found in a bag of old, unfinished quilt squares that a friend bought at a thrift shop. I used reproduction prints that look like the fabrics my mother and grandmother used to make aprons. Many quilt shops sell packets of fat quarters (18" x 22" pieces) of reproduction fabrics. The fat-quarter packets give you a good selection of prints and more than enough fabric for the butterflies and corner-stones.

Color photo on page 46.

Project Information at a Glance

Finished Quilt Size:	42½" x 53"
Finished Block Size:	9" x 9"
Number of Blocks to Make:	12
Finished Sashing Width:	1½"
Finished Outer Border Width:	6"

Materials: 44"-wide fabric

1 yd. light tone-on-tone print for background

5 fat quarters in a variety of print scales for butterflies, cornerstones, and corner squares

1⅜ yds. lavender for sashing, border, and binding

1¾ yds. for backing (includes 8" for sleeve)*

47" x 57" piece of batting

1 package water-soluble stabilizer (Solvy, Avalon, or Aqua-Solv)

Freezer paper

If your fabric has 45" of usable width, 1¾ yds. is sufficient. If your fabric has less usable width, you will need to buy 2½ yds. and piece the backing.

Cutting

Fabric	No. of Pieces	Size to Cut	Placement
Tone-on-tone	12	10½" x 10½"	Background
Fat quarters	12	7" x 9"	Butterflies
	6	2" x 2"	Cornerstones
	4	6½" x 6½"	Corner squares
Lavender	17	2" x 9½"	Sashing
	2	6½" x 30½"	Border (top & bottom)
	2	6½" x 41"	Border (sides)
	5	2" x 42"	Binding
Stabilizer	12	7" x 9"	

Block Assembly

1. Follow the directions for "Blind Appliqué" on pages 14–18 to make 12 butterflies.
2. Press the 10½" background squares diagonally to provide a placement guide for the butterflies. Position each butterfly on a background square; pin in place.
3. Make a plastic template to mark the stitching lines in the butterfly. With a chalk-wheel marker, mark the stitching lines on each butterfly, including the antennae.

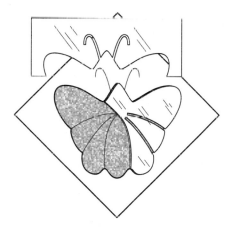

If you plan to use a programmed decorative stitch, such as the buttonhole stitch I used on my quilt, it's not necessary to stitch the appliqué to the background fabric first with a blind-hem stitch and invisible thread. Because the butterfly pattern is a simple one-piece appliqué, you can stitch it directly onto the background fabric. I used a heavy thread (#12 pearl cotton) and a size 80/12 topstitching needle to create a hand-stitched look.

4. On a sample piece of fabric, adjust the stitch length and width until you like the look of the straight and decorative stitches. (I used a length of 3mm for the straight stitch, and a length and width of 3.5mm for the buttonhole stitch).
5. Straight stitch the antennae and interior lines of each butterfly. Pull the threads to the wrong side of the background fabric, tie them in a knot with the bobbin thread, and clip, leaving 1" tails.
6. Buttonhole stitch around the outside edge of each butterfly. Pull the threads to the back, tie, and clip the tails.
7. Press the appliqués and trim the blocks to 9½" x 9½", carefully centering the butterfly in each block.

Quilt Assembly

1. Arrange the blocks into 4 rows of 3 blocks each, with two 2" x 9½" sashing strips between the blocks. Join the blocks and sashing strips to make a row.

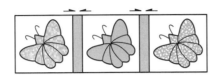

Make 4 rows.

2. Join three 2" x 9½" sashing strips and two 2" x 2" cornerstones to make a sashing row.

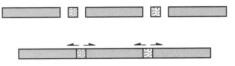

Make 3 rows.

3. Join the rows of blocks and sashing, pinning at the cornerstones to match the seams. Press.

4. Add the 6½" x 41" border strips to the sides of the quilt top. Stitch a 6½" x 6½" corner square to each end of the 6½" x 30½" border strips. Add the top and bottom border strips with corner squares to the quilt top.

Finishing

1. Layer the quilt top with batting and backing; pin-baste every 3".
2. Quilt by hand or machine. I quilted the quilt on page 46 by machine, stitching in-the-ditch of the sashing strips. I outlined the butterflies and stitched the design lines, then stipple quilted the background in each block. I quilted a smaller butterfly design in the border.
3. Attach the binding and add the sleeve.

Border quilting design

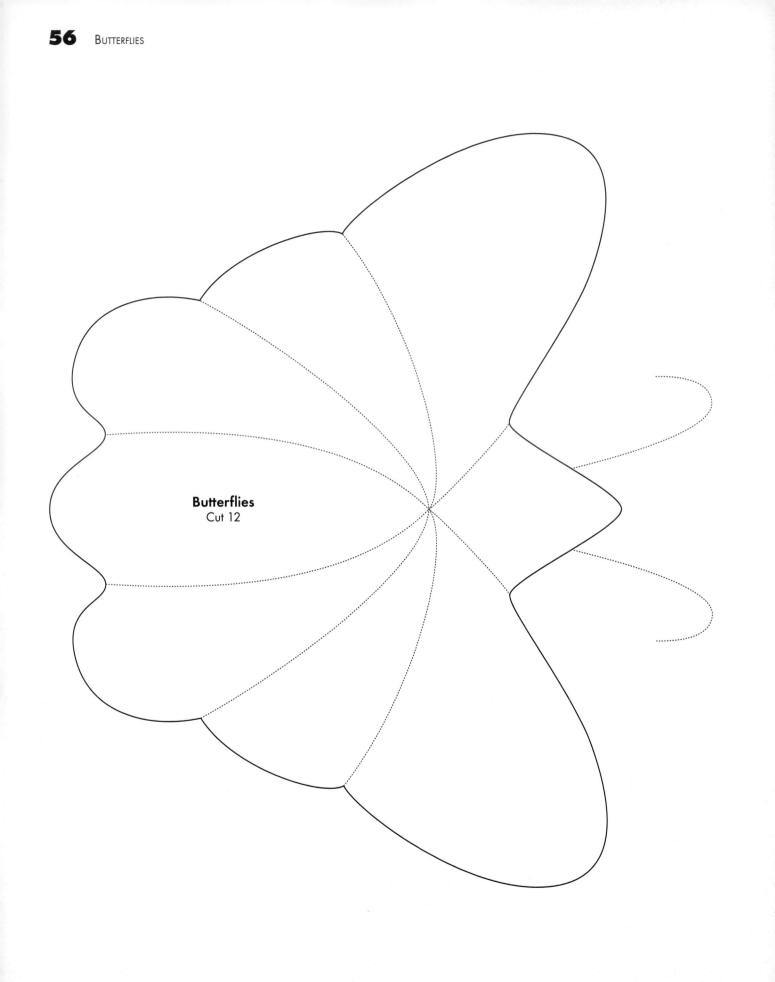

Butterflies
Cut 12

Tulip Time

Tulips remind me of spring in the Skagit Valley in the state of Washington. The hundreds of acres of tulips bring crowds of tourists to this rural farm community, causing traffic jams beyond belief. With this quilt, I tried to capture the shapes and colors of the season.

When planning an appliqué that features flowers, look for a fabric that has various shades and color changes. Hand-dyed fabric often has these traits.

This project is stitched using the blind-appliqué method, but it can be done upside-down or fused as well. If you use the upside-down method, turn to page 45 to see various ways of finishing the raw edges with programmed decorative stitches.

Color photo on page 44.

Project Information at a Glance	
Finished Quilt Size:	42½" x 42½"
Finished Block Size:	10" x 10"
Number of Blocks to Make:	4
Finished Sashing Width:	1½"
Finished Inner Border Widths:	2" and 1"
Finished Outer Border Width:	1½"

Materials: 44"-wide fabric

1⅜ yds. textured blue print for background

1 yd. multicolored or hand-dyed print for tulips, sashing, outer border, and binding

⅜ yd. green for leaves, stems, and 1" inner border

⅜ yd. lavender for 2" inner border

1⅝ yds. for backing (includes 8" for sleeve)*

1 package water-soluble stabilizer (Solvy, Avalon, or Aqua-Solv)

Freezer paper

47" x 47" square of lightweight cotton batting

*If your fabric has 44" of usable width, 1⅝ yds. is sufficient. If your fabric has less usable width, you will need to buy 2½ yds. and piece the backing.

Cutting

Fabric	No. of Pieces	Size to Cut	2nd Cut	Placement
Blue	4	11½" x 11½"		Background
	2	20⅜" x 20⅜"	◩	Setting triangles
Multi	12	2½" x 4"		Tulip appliqué
	2	2" x 10½"		Sashing
	1	2" x 22"		Sashing
	9	2" x width of fabric		Outer border and binding
Green	8	2" x 6"		Leaf appliqué
	1	1½" x 20"		Stems
	2	1½" x 26"		1" inner border
	2	1½" x 28"		1" inner border
Lavender	2	2½" x 22"		2" inner border
	2	2½" x 26"		2" inner border

◩ Cut the squares once diagonally.

Block Assembly

 Make a paper window the shape of the outer and inner tulip petals to help you find the perfect piece of fabric for each section of the flower.

1. Follow the directions for "Blind Appliqué" on pages 14–18 to make 4 tulip appliqués.
2. Press the background squares twice diagonally to provide a placement guide for the tulips. Position the tulips on the background squares; pin and stitch. Trim the blocks to 10½" x 10½", carefully centering the appliqué.

Quilt Assembly

1. Join 2 blocks with a 2" x 10½" sashing strip between. Press the seam allowances toward the sashing strip. Repeat with the remaining 2 blocks. Join the rows with the 2" x 22" sashing strip between.

2. Add the 2½" x 22" inner border strips to opposite sides of the quilt top. Add the 2½" x 26" inner border strips to the remaining sides of the quilt top. Press.

3. Add the 1½" x 26" inner border strips, followed by the 1½" x 28" inner border strips.

4. Mark the midpoints on the long edges of 2 setting triangles. Mark the midpoints on opposite edges of the quilt top. Pin the triangles to the quilt top, matching the midpoints; stitch. Repeat with the remaining triangles on the other sides of the quilt top. Press and trim.

Remember to place the long bias edge of the background triangle under the straight-grain edge of the border when stitching.

5. Measure the quilt top crosswise through the center and cut 2 border strips to that measurement. Add the outer border strips to the top and bottom. Measure the quilt top lengthwise through the center and cut 2 border strips to that measurement. Add the outer border strips to the sides.

Finishing

1. Layer the quilt top with batting and backing. Pin-baste or tack every 3".

2. Hand or machine quilt. I machine quilted the quilt on page 44 in-the-ditch of the sashing and borders and around each tulip. I used a walking foot and a variegated #12 pearl cotton with a 80/12 topstitching needle to stitch around each tulip. The edge of the walking foot was my stitching guide.

3. Divide each setting triangle into 5 parts by marking 4 evenly spaced spots on each outer edge with pins. Using a Hera marker or chalk wheel, make a line from each outer point to the midpoint of each triangle's long side. Stitch from the outside in, and back to the outside edge. The binding will secure the ends of the thread.

4. Attach the binding and add the sleeve.

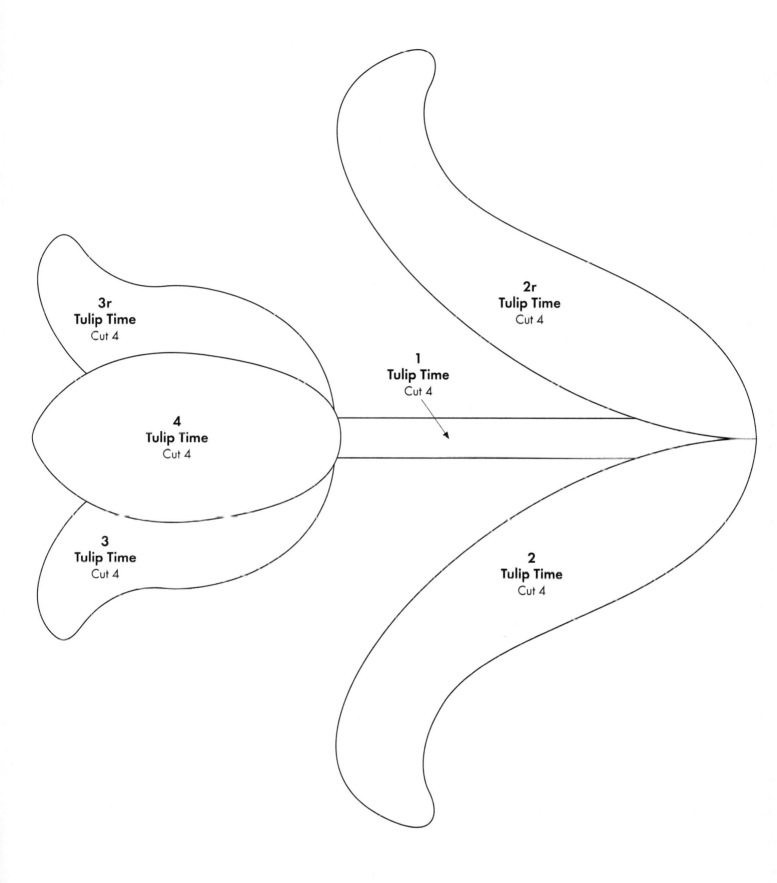

3r
Tulip Time
Cut 4

2r
Tulip Time
Cut 4

1
Tulip Time
Cut 4

4
Tulip Time
Cut 4

3
Tulip Time
Cut 4

2
Tulip Time
Cut 4

Rose of Sharon

The Rose of Sharon pattern has many design variations. I created this traditional block by surrounding a center flower with four stems and four corner flowers. You can make this quilt using any of the three appliqué methods explained on pages 11–26. The quilt shown on page 47 is appliquéd using the upside-down method. If you use the blind method, trace all of the pattern pieces, adding a ¼" extension on each piece that will tuck under another piece.

Color photo on page 47.

Project Information at a Glance	
Finished Quilt Size:	43½" x 43½"
Finished Block Size:	16" x 16"
Number of Blocks to Make:	4
Finished Sashing Width:	3"
Finished Center Cornerstone:	3" x 3"
Finished Border Width:	4"
Finished Corner Squares:	4" x 4"

Materials: 44"-wide fabric

1 yd. textured print for block background

⅞ yd. green for leaves and stems

⅜ yd. purple for flowers, center cornerstone, and corner squares

1⅜ yds. multicolored print for flowers, sashing, and border

⅛ yd. or scraps of orange for flower centers

1⅝ yds. for backing (includes 8" for sleeve)*

48" x 48" piece of lightweight cotton batting

4 squares, each 16" x 16", of iron-on, tear-away stabilizer (Press 'N Tear or Totally Stable)

If your fabric has 45" of usable width, 1⅝ yds. is sufficient. If your fabric has less usable width, you will need to buy 2½ yds. and piece the backing.

Cutting

Fabric	No. of Pieces	Size to Cut	Placement
Textured print	4	17½" x 17½"	Background
Green	4	15" x 15"	Leaves, stems, and base of corner flower
Purple	4	6" x 6"	Outer ring of center flower
	1	3½" x 3½"	Center cornerstone
	4	4½" x 4½"	Corner squares
Multi	4	4" x 4"	Inner ring of center flower
	16	3" x 5"	Corner flowers
	4	3½" x 16½"	Sashing
	4	4½" x 35½"	Border
	5	2" x 42"	Binding
Orange	20	2" x 2"	Flower centers

Block Assembly

1. Follow the directions for "Upside-Down Appliqué" on pages 22–26 to make 4 appliqué blocks. Satin stitch the pieces in this order:
   - centers of all flowers
   - blossom of corner flowers and inner ring of center flower
   - leaves, stem, and base on corner flowers
   - outer ring of center flower
2. Press and trim each appliqué block to 16½" x 16½", carefully centering the appliqué.

Quilt Assembly

1. Join 2 blocks and a sashing strip to make a row. Make another row.

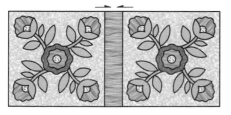

Make 2 rows.

2. Join the 2 remaining sashing strips and the center cornerstone.

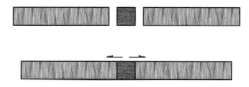

Make 1 strip.

3. Join the rows of blocks with the sashing strip between.

4. Add a border strip to opposite sides of the quilt top. Stitch a corner square to each end of the remaining border strips. Add the border strips with corner squares to the top and bottom of the quilt top.

Finishing

1. Layer the quilt top with batting and backing; pin-baste.

2. Quilt by hand or by machine. I machine quilted the quilt on page 47 by first stitching in-the-ditch around the squares. Then I outlined the appliqués and filled in the background with elongated stipple quilting. Use one of the leaves from the appliqué pattern to make a template for the quilting in the sashing and borders.

3. Attach the binding and add the sleeve.

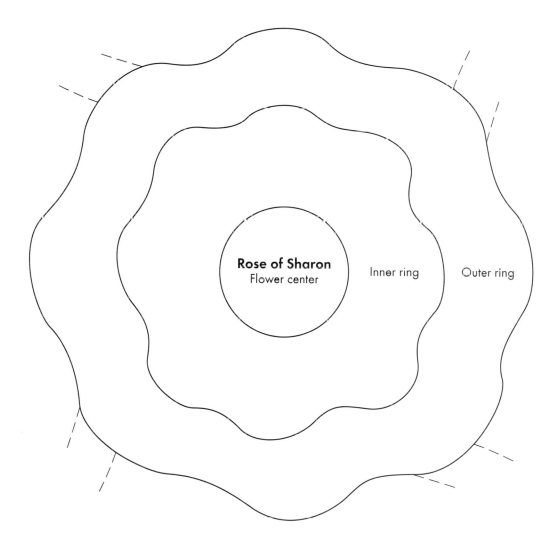

Rose of Sharon
Flower center   Inner ring   Outer ring

Rose of Sharon
Flower blossom

Flower center

Flower base

Leaf

Leaf

Leaf

Stem

Dream Creatures

These imaginary creatures provide you with a wonderful opportunity to work with more complex appliqué shapes and to test your satin-stitching skills. I made my quilt using the up-side-down method, but you can fuse it if you prefer.

I originally planned to give just the cat spots using programmed decorative stitches, but I quickly decided to decorate all the creatures. The satin stitching and decorative stitching are done with rayon thread. Let your imagination guide you when you choose fabrics, threads, and stitches.

Color photo on page 48.

Project Information at a Glance	
Finished Quilt Size:	35½" x 47"
Finished Block Size:	10½" x 10½"
Number of Blocks to Make:	6
Finished Sashing Width:	1"
Finished Border Width:	5½"

Materials: 44"-wide fabric

¾ yd. green fabric for background

6 squares, each 10" x 10", in varied bright colors for creatures

6 squares, each 10" x 10", of iron-on, tear-away stabilizer (Press 'N Tear or Totally Stable)

⅓ yd. orange for sashing

¾ yd. multicolored print for border

¼ yd. purple for binding

1¾ yds. for backing (includes 8" for sleeve)

40" x 51" piece of lightweight cotton batting

Cutting

Fabric	No. of Pieces	Size to Cut	Placement
Green	6	12" x 12"	Background
Orange	3	1½" x 11"	Sashing
	4	1½" x 22½"	Sashing
	2	1½" x 36"	Sashing
Multi	2	6" x 36"	Outer border (sides)
	2	6" x 35½"	Outer border (top & bottom)
Purple	4	2" x 42"	Binding

Block Assembly

1. Follow the directions for "Upside-Down Appliqué" on pages 22–26 to make 6 blocks.

 If you would like to use rayon thread for the satin stitching, choose 40-weight and use a 75/11 Embroidery needle. This needle has a larger eye, which prevents the thread from shredding and breaking.

2. On a stabilized scrap of fabric, play with your programmed decorative stitches until you find single patterns that you like. (If you have a computerized machine, you will be able to stitch a single pattern easily by setting the machine to stop after stitching one portion of the pattern.) Decorate your animals. Bring the thread ends to the back; tie and clip 1" tails.

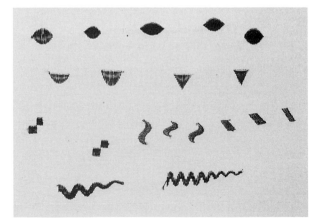

3. Remove the stabilizer and press the blocks. Trim each block to 11" x 11", carefully centering the appliqué.

Quilt Assembly

1. Arrange the blocks into 3 rows of 2 blocks each, with a 1½" x 11" sashing strip between each pair of blocks. Join the blocks and sashing strips into rows. Join the rows, with a 1½" x 22½" sashing strip between each row. Add a 1½" x 22½" sashing strip to the top and bottom edges of the quilt top.

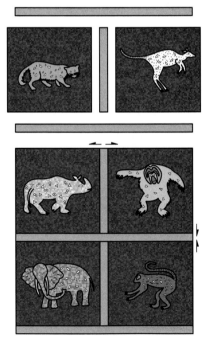

2. Add the 1½" x 36" sashing strips to the sides of the quilt top.

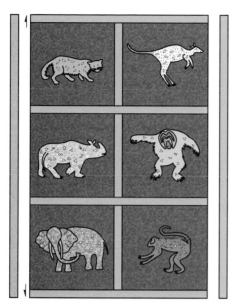

3. Add the 6" x 36" border strips to the sides of the quilt top. Add the 6" x 35½" border strips to the top and bottom of the quilt top.

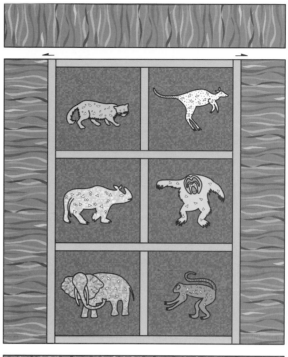

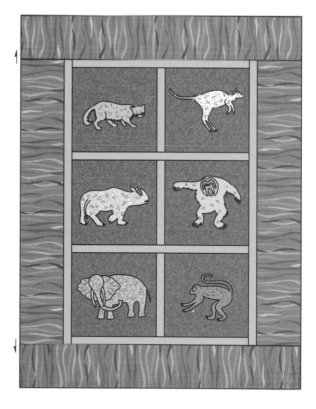

Finishing

1. Layer the quilt top with batting and backing; pin-baste.
2. Quilt by hand or machine. I machine quilted the quilt on page 48 by first stitching in-the-ditch on both sides of the sashing. I then outlined the creatures and filled in the background of the blocks with a free-motion, meandering vine pattern.

   If your border fabric has a design, use it as your quilting pattern. I used the curvy lines on the fabric to quilt the borders.
3. Bind the edges and add a sleeve. Your creatures are ready to hang!

Quilting design

Dream Creatures
Cat

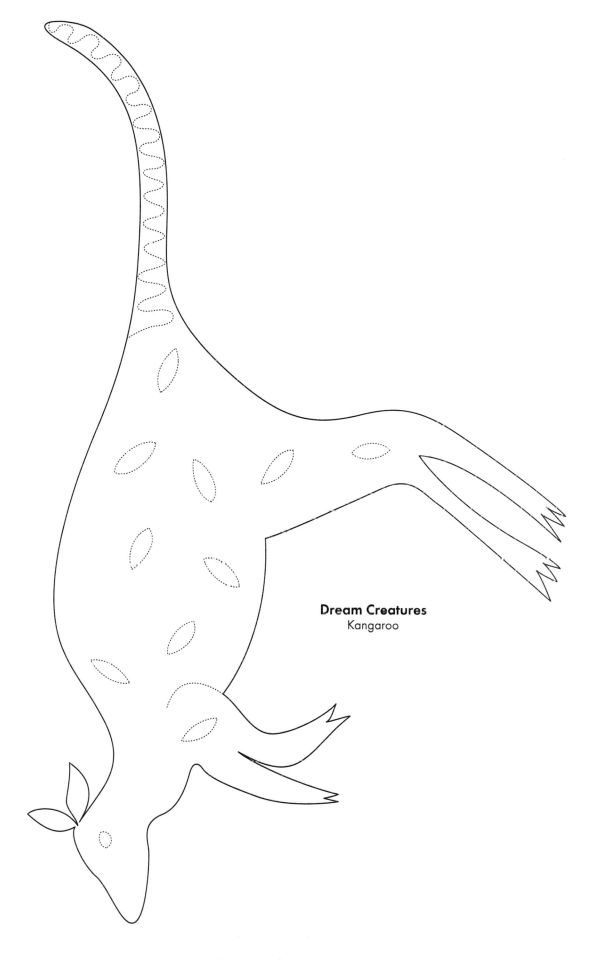

Dream Creatures
Kangaroo

Dream Creatures
Rhino

Dream Creatures
Ape

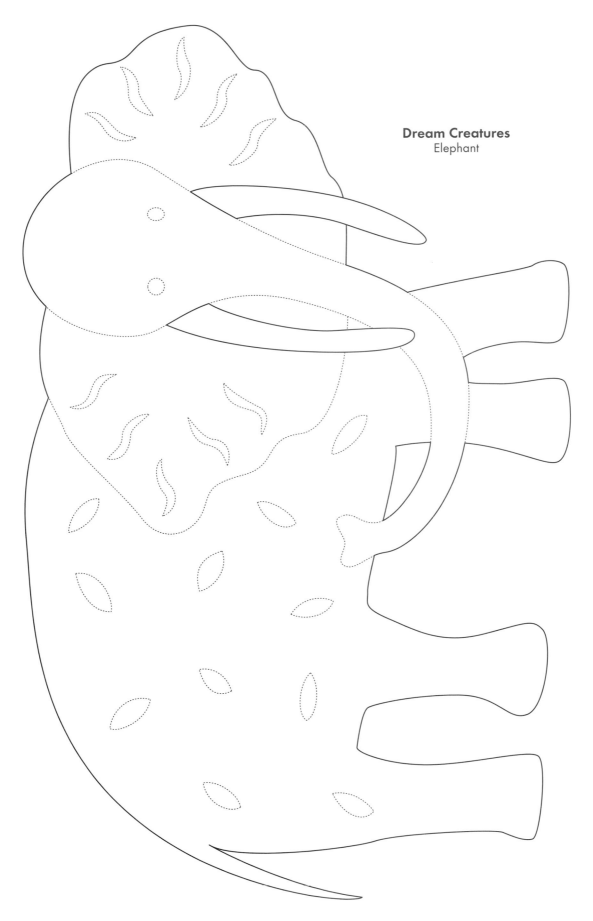

Dream Creatures
Elephant

Dream Creatures
Monkey

Star-Spangled Night

This project uses lamé fabrics and the fused appliqué method. Lamé is ideal for a wall hanging that won't be handled a great deal. Look for a lamé that has a knit backing. If you can only find tissue lamé, without a backing, press a lightweight, iron-on interfacing to the wrong side of the lamé before using the fabric for the appliqué pieces. The interfacing will stabilize the lamé and keep the cut edges from fraying. Use as many stars and different lamé colors as you like. Be creative!

Color photo on page 43.

Project Information at a Glance

Finished Quilt Size: 30" x 38"

Materials: 44"-wide fabric

1 1/4 yds. midnight teal for background
1/4 yd. each of various colors of lamé
1 yd. Steam-A-Seam 2 Double Stick
1 3/8 yds. for backing (includes 8" for sleeve)
1/4 yd. stripe for binding
34" x 42" piece of lightweight batting

Cutting

Fabric	No. of Pieces	Size to Cut	Placement
Teal	1	32" x 40"	Background
Lamé	Your choice	Moon & stars	Appliqué
Stripe	4	2" x 42"	Binding

Quilt Assembly and Finishing

1. Trace the moon and as many stars as you like on one paper side of Steam-A-Seam 2 Double Stick.

Paper

You may find it easier to make a plastic template for each star and trace around the templates. Cut the shapes apart, leaving at least ¼" between pieces. (Do not cut on the lines.)

2. Remove the paper from the other side of the Steam-A-Seam 2 on each shape. Finger-press the sticky side to the wrong side of the lamé fabric.

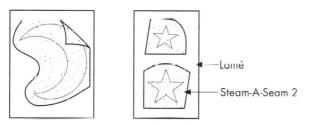

Lamé

Steam-A-Seam 2

3. Cut out the appliqué pieces, using the tracing lines as a guide.

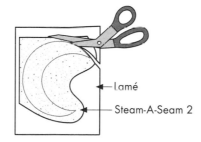

Lamé

Steam-A-Seam 2

4. Remove the remaining paper liner from the shapes and place them on the background fabric. The sticky back of the fusible web will allow you to reposition the pieces until you are happy with the arrangement.

5. Set your iron on the permanent-press setting. Fuse the shapes in place, using a press cloth to protect the lamé. (Placing a hot iron directly on lamé can damage its finish.) If you follow the directions on the package, the appliqué pieces do not need to be stitched.

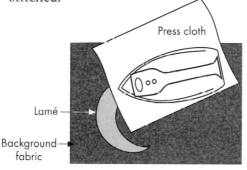

Press cloth

Lamé

Background fabric

6. Because I love to use decorative threads, I stitched the moon and stars using light-weight metallic and iridescent threads. Test the stitch and tension by stitching a star on a sample of background fabric. Use a 70/10 or 80/12 metallic needle with lightweight metallic thread and lightweight polyester bobbin thread in the bobbin. Do not use a tight satin stitch; it will cut the lamé. Set the zigzag stitch to 2mm wide and 1mm long and follow the directions for satin stitching. (See page 30 to stitch perfect points.) At these settings, the stitch will not form a solid line.

7. Layer the quilt top with batting and backing; pin-baste.

8. Outline-quilt each star and moon. Stitch curved lines from the top of the quilt to one of the stars, making it look like a meteor. Quilt repeating small star shapes in the background. I used a star fabric for the backing and quilted from the back, following the design lines. To stitch upside down, put the metallic thread in the bobbin.

9. Attach the binding and add the sleeve. Sweet dreams!

Star-Spangled Night
Star

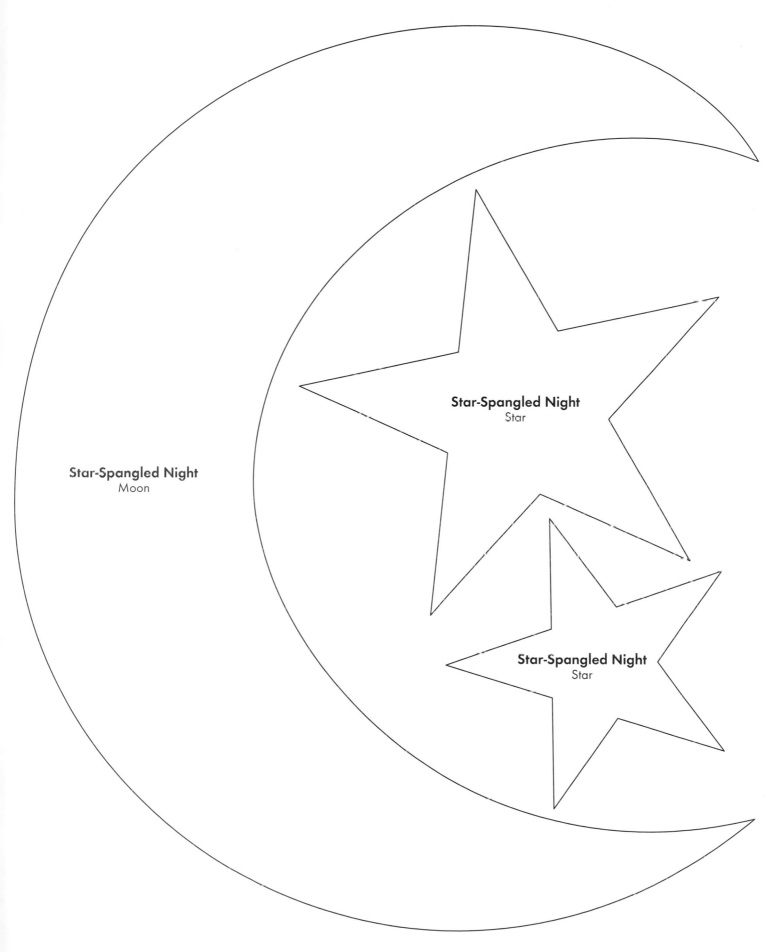

Star-Spangled Night
Star

Star-Spangled Night
Moon

Star-Spangled Night
Star

Meet the Author

Maurine Leander Noble is a former home-economics teacher who is addicted to quilting and sewing machines. She teaches machine appliqué and machine-quilting techniques, specializing in using decorative threads. Her books *Machine Quilting Made Easy* and *Machine Quilting with Decorative Threads* (co-authored with Elizabeth Hendricks) are published by Martingale & Company. Seattle, Washington, is her home, but teaching keeps her traveling locally and nationally.

Suggested Books

Basic Quiltmaking

Your First Quilt Book (or it should be!) by Carol Doak (That Patchwork Place, Inc.)

Color

Color: The Quilter's Guide by Christine Barnes (That Patchwork Place, Inc.)

The Magical Effects of Color by Joen Wolfrom (C&T Publishing)

Appliqué

Basic Quiltmaking Techniques for Hand Appliqué by Mimi Dietrich (Martingale & Company)

Appliqué: 12 Easy Ways by Elly Sienkiewicz (C&T Publishing)

Mastering Machine Appliqué by Harriet Hargrave (C&T Publishing)

The Easy Art of Appliqué by Mimi Dietrich and Roxi Eppler (That Patchwork Place, Inc.)

Hand Quilting

How to Improve Your Quilting Stitch by Ami Simms (Mallery Press)

Loving Stitches by Jeana Kimball (That Patchwork Place, Inc.)

Machine Quilting

Machine Quilting Made Easy by Maurine Noble (That Patchwork Place, Inc.)

Machine Quilting with Decorative Threads by Maurine Noble & Elizabeth Hendricks (Martingale & Company)

Heirloom Machine Quilting by Harriet Hargrave (C&T Publishing)

Bindings

Happy Endings by Mimi Dietrich (That Patchwork Place, Inc.)

A Fine Finish by Cody Mazuran (That Patchwork Place, Inc.)